HOW CHET BAKER DIED

Poems

BARRY GIFFORD

SEVEN STORIES PRESS
New York • Oakland • London

SEVEN STORIES PRESS
140 Watts Street
New York, NY 10013
www.sevenstories.com

College professors and high school and middle school teachers
may order free examination copies of Seven Stories Press titles.
Visit https://www.sevenstories.com/pg/resources-academics
or email academics@sevenstories.com.

Library of Congress Cataloging-in-Publication Data

Names: Gifford, Barry, 1946- author.
Title: How Chet Baker died : poems / Barry Gifford.
Description: New York : Seven Stories Press, [2021]
Identifiers: LCCN 2021045956 | ISBN 9781644211540 (hardcover) | ISBN
    9781644211557 (ebook)
Subjects: LCGFT: Poetry.
Classification: LCC PS3557.I283 H683 2021 | DDC 811/.54--dc23
LC record available at https://lccn.loc.gov/2021045956

ACKNOWLEDGMENTS

Some of these poems have previously appeared in the following publications:
Amerarcana (San Francisco), *The Chicagoist* (Chicago), *Exquisite Corpse*
(Baltimore), *Handshake Editions* (Paris), *Nexos* (Mexico City), *Little Star*
(New York), *The New Yorker* (New York), *The Lemuria Bookstore Newsletter*
(Jackson, Ms.), *Granta* (Spain), and in a limited edition entitled *New York,
1960* (Chicago: Curbside Splendor, 2016).

Title page drawing of Chet Baker by Barry Gifford.

For Jim Harrison and Al Young after the fact
and for Peter Maravelis in the moment

"Time does not occur to the king."

—Rumored to have been the last
words of the King of Dahomey
prior to his strangulation
by the hands of his wives.

"There is no control over memory."

—Jean Rhys

CONTENTS

HOW CHET BAKER DIED

Blood Moon in February

Here I am wasting time again
writing poems to keep myself company—
The Chinese masters of the T'ang dynasty
thought the same, but mostly
they were rural government functionaries
or already collecting a pension,
out of favor with the emperor—
So they drank rice wine
and kept their opinions to themselves,
sneaking hidden meanings into poems
they knew only a very few people
would read during their lifetime—
Who cares about a barking dog
nobody sees, or what kind of bird
sings just before light—
Only in darkness do my thoughts
cohere, vagrant ghosts
passing in dreams, difficult
if not impossible to find again—
Perhaps there never was anything
to worry about, and now know
when the dog barks or the bird sings
there aren't any thoughts
worth keeping

New York, 1960

What could she be thinking,
this girl carrying a suitcase
with her left hand and a bag
with her right?
Wearing a sleeveless summer dress
walking alone on a busy
(probably) Manhattan street,
she looks at the sidewalk,
hair covering her right eye.
Her dress is decorated with daffodils.
Is she moving? Leaving town?
Did she break up with her boyfriend?
Did he blacken her hidden eye?
She's young, early twenties,
with a good figure. The photographer
who took her picture didn't know her,
thought she was kind of pretty,
perhaps tried to pick her up, offered
to carry the suitcase, buy her a cup
of coffee. Fifty-three years ago.
She took a bus back to Ohio, worked
in a dentist's office, married him,
had two kids, divorced. Her son
joined the Navy, lives in San Diego.
Daughter's in Idaho, married
to a metallurgist. The dentist died
from a self-administered drug overdose.
Tonight she's thinking about that year
and a half in New York. What happened
to Eddie? Or his handsome friend, Phil?
Phil was from Altoona, Pennsylvania.
How could she remember that? Raining
here, mid-August in Dayton. This girl
in the photograph, that girl.

The Disappeared

People disappear all the time,
people with whom you've done
or planned to do business,
people you used to see at the bar,
walking past your house, been in love with,
lived with, even married.
The disappearing Mexicans, Brazilians,
Italians, a few French, some Russians.
How is it they disappear so easily,
suddenly, completely? Out of indifference,
dislike, imprisonment, insanity, denial,
death, they're gone—some you miss,
some you don't, but it's so often
a mystery. You might hear about them
in the news, from a friend, think you've
spotted them hurrying by on a busy street,
or receive a birthday card without
a return address from someone you
met on a ship. People who don't
need you any more or think you don't
need them—they're usually right.
No, I can't forget them, the ones
who've gotten lost. After all,
I've gotten lost myself, and I know
where I am even if they don't.

Big Words

for Arthur Okazaki

What's my old friend
Arthur Okazaki doing
today in New Orleans?
Here in San Francisco
it's a gloomy January day
clouds everywhere, even
on the ground almost
like it used to be when
I first got here nearly
fifty years ago—
Arthur sent me a photo,
two photos pasted together
titled "Bomber" of a gas
station and an airplane
one overlapping the other—
Arthur's an artist, writer
and photographer who
will live to be a hundred
(he's almost there) like
his parents in Hawaii did—
Arthur was born and grew up
in Honolulu, he promised
to take me there to visit
Hotel Street but we never went,
now probably too late—
He's a great artist, a genius,
really, with a surprising
sense of humor who knows jazz,
women, baseball and how to
make a great gin martini—
What more to ask
of a man? I forgot
to say he's also generous

(with money, time) and never
gives advice (at least not to me),
which is enough to qualify
him as a sort of saint—
A bow to you, Okazaki-san,
on this rainy day and
every other for so long
as we still have them—
I wish I had a better poem
to send you and that
we two were sitting in
your kitchen with martinis
listening to Jackie McLean
or Sonny Stitt—Here
there are goldfinches
in the kumquat tree,
when it rains they hide
behind the leaves,
black caps, white-striped tails—
their songs remind me of Eric Dolphy
on "Straight Ahead"—two months
ago in New York after listening
to George Mraz play his solo
I said to him, "There was a lot
of Dolphy in there," and he replied
Those are big words, man.

The Unconquered Flame

Both the actress Hedy Lamarr
and the writer Clarice Lispector,
outstanding beauties in their youth,
believed, as Lispector wrote,
"it was ugly to go out when one
was no longer young."
Still only in their forties,
they hid themselves away, wishing
to be remembered as they had been.
My mother, also a great beauty
into middle age, felt differently.
She was relieved, she said, to not
have to bear the burden of being
looked at. "I was frightened
by the thought of others wanting
to possess and destroy me."
Nevertheless, she never stopped
asking those closest to her
how she looked.
One night,
in the Bar Chicote in Madrid,
in the company of a famous
film director and an actress
considered by many to be among
the most beautiful women
in the world, I was admiring
a photograph on a wall
of Ava Gardner at her loveliest
drinking in Chicote
with Ernest Hemingway
when the actress asked me who
I thought was more beautiful,
she or Ava Gardner.
"What an impossible question!"

said the director. "Don't answer,"
he instructed. "If you choose Ava,
this one will hate you, and if you
choose her, she'll know you're lying."
I looked at the actress.
"Please lie," she said.

Ciao, Paloma

She stood and walked across the lawn
past the cottage and into the big house.
He stayed to watch the last of the sunset,
waiting for the flash of green.
When it was finally dark and there was
no moon and the fireflies appeared,
he got up and began walking toward the house.
He loved the Italian word for firefly,
lúcciola. She was like that, flickering
on and off from moment to moment.
As he approached the house, he could hear
her singing: *Vógliatemi bene, un bene
piccolino*. It's so strange, he thought,
life's so fast and time's too slow.
He stopped and watched the fireflies.

Ode to Jerry

My old friend Jerry Rosen
told me he used to stand
under the air conditioner
in the back of the room
at the Five Spot in New York
and listen to Monk, Coltrane,
Wilbur Ware and Shadow Wilson
every chance he got
for the six months that quartet
was together—"This was in 1957,
before Coltrane went out
on his own," Jerry said
"Trane learned about beauty
from Monk—just listen
to their recording of
'Ruby, My Dear'"
Shadow Wilson died in 1959,
Coltrane next, then Monk—
Now Jerry's gone, too.
I think about him every time
I hear "Ruby, My Dear"
It's a gift, recognizing beauty
in any form—Monk and Trane
were lucky to have had Jerry
listening to them

Mouth of the River

You came to me last night in a dream,
which is not unusual. Dead people
visit the living all the time and dreams
are a familiar and convenient avenue.
You rang my doorbell and asked me
to come with you to where you'd parked
your car. I could take your suitcase
and carry it back to the house while
you found a better place to park.
You looked good, your hair cut short
and very black, amber skin glowing,
smile white. You wore a green blouse
and a black skirt. Your visit was
a surprise, you had a few days off
from work, you said, and you wanted
to see me. You were neither young
nor old, about thirty-five, ten years
before your death. I left the door open
and followed you to your little red car.
The day was dark but the street well-lit.
I took your suitcase out of the car
and as you were getting into the driver's
seat you said, I'll be at the house
in a few minutes, then drove away.
I was happy you'd come but puzzled,
your driving all the way from Mexico City
without telling me you were coming.
What if I'd been out of town? As I walked
back to the house it started to rain.
I was wearing an old blue T-shirt
with holes in it and suddenly I got cold.
I left the front door open and built
a fire in the fireplace. You didn't come back.
I fell asleep in a chair. When I woke up

the fire was out and your suitcase was gone.
The door was still open and I went to close it
but before I did I looked outside. The sky
was beginning to get light and there was snow
on the ground. I thought about you on the beach
at Boca del Río, behind the Hotel Mocambo,
how long your hair was then. There was a band
and boys were dancing on the sand. This was
where your family would come when you were
a child, you told me, that's why I brought you here.

Women and Death

These days my poems
    are mostly about
        women and death
    in other words
      those who are gone
        It was Pessoa
      among others
  who suggested that
      memories
        are merely residue
  of what's best left
          forgotten
And Lady Pan
    victim of slander
    in the court
      of Ch'eng-ti
understood how
      dangerous
  to hold
      her dreams
  in such
    high regard

The Funeral

The second time we were in Grosseto—
it was for your mother's funeral—
we stayed in a hotel where, in the bar
on the second floor, I ordered a gin martini.
The woman bartender had no idea how to
make it. In Italy, you explained, it's
called a martini dry, to differentiate it
from plain vermouth. The bartender
served me a glass filled with half parts
of white vermouth and gin, which, of course,
is not even close to being a martini dry.
Bartenders in the Grand Hotel in Rome
make them perfectly, but we were in small,
unsophisticated Grosseto, which had been
described to me by my friend Enrico Ghezzi
as the ugliest town in Tuscany. It isn't
pretty, but I like the old prison walls
that were left standing in the center.
Don't drink it, you said, you'll get sick.
The bartender studied us as if she thought
we were from Outer Space. My girlfriend
grew up here, I told the bartender. We're here
for her mother's funeral. The woman's expression
of disapproval was unchanged. Pay her and let's go,
you said. Don't you want something to drink?
I asked. You shook your head and I put more
than enough money on the bar. As we were leaving,
I looked back and saw the bartender hold the glass
briefly to her nose, then dump the contents
into the sink. It was even hotter in our room
than it was outside. My mother would never
enter this hotel, you told me. She said
it was where my father brought his whores.

Last Night's Dream

In last night's dream I went back to see you
I found you on a bad street in Mexico City
working as a prostitute
You didn't want me to look at you
You'd lost your job, had no money
Come with me, I said, I'll take care of you
You wouldn't let me touch you
No, you said, it won't be any use,
and anyway, you know I'm dead
I hung around out of sight and watched you
solicit strangers on the street,
men walking, men in cars
You came around a corner and spotted me
Leave me alone you said, it's too late
You still looked good, your hair was clean
and black but a couple of your teeth were missing
and your clothes were soiled
You walked quickly toward another street
Don't follow me, you shouted
I remembered that you had a photograph
of me on a wall in your house,
one I'd never seen before
I asked you where it was from,
who'd taken it, where you'd gotten it
I made it, you said, out of photographs
of other people, it was difficult
and it took me a very long time

Passing Acquaintance

Ultra Violet died yesterday.
She was seventy-eight.
We met seventeen years ago
at the bar of the Westbury Hotel
in New York. She was alone,
wearing a mink coat and a pin
that spelled her name in diamonds.
Even at sixty-one she was beautiful.
I'd heard of her early life with Dalí,
and later years with Warhol.
For the moment, I was by myself,
about to meet someone in front
of the hotel. She saw me come in
and sit next to her at the bar,
which was uncrowded at four-thirty
in the afternoon. She was smoking
a cigarette. I ordered a martini,
Bombay Sapphire, very dry, two olives.
Her glass was empty. May I buy you
a drink? I asked. Of course, she said,
the same as yours. She had a French accent.
I noticed her pin. Should I know you?
I asked. You should, she answered,
at least twenty, perhaps thirty years ago.
Our drinks came. Even then, she said,
who knows?

At Apollinaire's Grave, Pére-Lachaise

A black and white cat
crawls off as I approach
Apollinaire's grave is well-kept
with many new flowers
planted in rows along
either side, two vases
filled with pink roses
in fresh water
Kostrowitzky was his name
a Pole with one strange eye
and a derby hat
A crooked stone, eight
feet high, marks his place
and Jacqueline's
Inscribed at the foot
in the shape of a heart
are the words:
Mon coeur pareil à
une flammere reversée
The black and white cat
returns, looks quickly
at me and lies down
on *flammere*

At Ezra Pound's Grave, San Michele

This is the Day of the Dead
in Italy, ten years to
the day of your death
Here you are on an island
as you were in life
a paradise for mourners
Your thirst for beauty
brought you to the right place
Venice is a world beyond
you could see that clearly
Just as this is the last sun
of the year, or nearly

Passage on a Slow Freighter

Blaise Cendrars wrote,
Today I am perhaps the happiest man
in the world. I have everything
I don't want.
When I was younger, I could not
have understood this feeling.
Now, three years shy of seventy,
it makes sense, a sentiment
I share, having shed the pride
of both possessiveness and, worse,
false necessity. No longer
important to fool myself
or believe my own lies.
It's the sparrow on the window sill
on a darkening afternoon—
that we both can smell
the fast-approaching rain
is all the belonging I need.

For Yosano Akiko, whose heart was like the sun

Forty-two years ago we were in Japan
in the countryside staying at
the house of an old poet
Outside the window of our room
on the second floor a bird
sang throughout the night
The next morning I asked our host
what kind of bird it could have been
There are no songbirds in
this part of the country, he said,
a bird was singing in your dream
Later you told me that you
had heard it, too
Between notes, you said, there was
a crackling sound in its throat
Why didn't you say this before, I asked
It would have been impolite
to contradict our host, you said
Who knows what significance
this bird's song may have to him
Perhaps he believes it's the voice
of someone dear to him who has died
or gone away long ago
Things are different here
we are in Japan

Approaching the Forbidden City

When I was 20 years old I saw a girl on Webster Street
in Oakland Chinatown inspecting apples at a produce stand.
She looked like Anna May Wong, the actress who was in
Shanghai Express and other films in the 1920s and '30s,
petite, cat-like, with black bangs and long fingers.
I went up to her and asked, Did anyone ever tell you
how much you resemble the actress Anna May Wong?
My name is Anna, she said, and asked, Is she very pretty?
She was, I said, she's been dead for several years.
She was born in Chinatown in Los Angeles. I was born
in Hong Kong, said the girl, my family moved to Oakland
when I was three years old. I'm 21 now. I work nights
as a hostess at the Silver Dragon restaurant. Maybe
you'll come in sometime. Tuesday through Saturday.
These apples aren't so good, she said. Thanks for
telling me about Anna May Wong, I'll check her out.
We shook hands, she smiled, and walked away.
I remembered Anna May Wong in the silent film *Mr. Wu*,
in which she played an attendant to and confidante of
the daughter of Mr. Wu, ruler of a Chinese province,
played by Lon Chaney. Louise Dresser played his daughter,
and of course neither of them looked at all Chinese.
Anna May Wong was much prettier and perkier than
Louise Dresser, she stole every scene she was in.
I'd been to the Silver Dragon once but hadn't gone back
because the food was not very good, but I knew
I'd try it again even though Mr. Wu killed his daughter
because she fell in love with a white man.

Catastrophe at the Grocery Store

Rain was in the forecast for the first time
in months, it was a gloomy morning,
so I walked to the corner grocery store
to look at the Eritrean women who work there
They're all beautiful, always smiling,
they wear sparkling jewelry, black hair
piled high and perfectly arranged,
teeth shining brightly, and dresses
so colorful I expect them to burst into flame
Suddenly the lights went out, not only
in the grocery store but all over
the neighborhood—While we waited for the power
to come back on so that the cash registers
could function, I told the Eritrean woman
at whose counter I was standing
that the last device on which Thomas Edison,
inventor of the electric light,
was working before he died
was a machine that would enable the living
to contact the dead—The cashier's smile
disappeared, her mouth dropped open
and the pupils of her eyes dilated wildly
Did this machine work? she asked
I don't think he got that far, I said
After his death his heirs supposedly
destroyed his notes on the project
in order to protect the financial stability
of his company, General Electric—
they didn't want word of his research
to become public—also, Edison's son
was planning to run for governor
of New Jersey and they didn't want
to embarrass him for fear this information
would sabotage his campaign

The lights came back on and the registers
began ringing again
I paid the cashier for coffee, bananas
and bread and left the store
A little rain was falling now
I shouldn't have upset the Eritrean woman,
I thought, by telling her about Edison's
last experiment—I wanted to see her smile
when I went into the grocery store
It lit up the room

After Life

In the dream my dear friend Tita Sorcia
whom I had been told three years ago
had died in Mexico City was revealed
to still be alive in a remote mountain village
in the state of Veracruz residing among
Totonac Indians who are distant relatives
What is she doing there? I asked the person
who called to tell me this news
Weaving baskets with other women
of the village to sell to tourists, he said
Why would she want people to think
she was dead? I asked. Who can know?
he answered. Didn't you ever wish to disappear
without warning, to become invisible, to leave
everyone and everything in the present behind?
When I woke up I pictured Tita as I knew her
lovely as ever, well dressed, sitting at the bar
of a trendy restaurant in Roma Norte
sipping a martini, talking and laughing softly
in her shy way, showing her very white teeth
long black hair unfurled to her shoulders
She's made it easy on herself, I thought,
having already entered her afterlife
without explanation or having to die
to get there.

Remember

Remember in Odds Against Tomorrow
when Robert Ryan doesn't shoot the rabbit
he's waiting on a country road
for a car to pick him up
to take him to the city
to rob a bank with Harry Belafonte
and Ed Begley in a small
Pennsylvania town
Ryan's a racist, hates Harry,
and Begley's a crooked ex-cop
dumped from the force
The world will never again
look like it did in 1959
nothing's in black and white
any more—during the day
the sky's murky, at night
streets are wet, too dismal
for words so nobody speaks
buried behind their eyes
without time—it's what the movies
are about, nothing changes
no matter how often you see
this one Ryan misses his shot

March 17

St Patrick's Day
I watched Odd Man Out
to see Kathleen Sullivan
die alongside
her beloved, gravely
wounded Johnny McQueen
snow coming down
on their heads
by the harbor
she fires two shots
forcing the police
to fire back
She didn't die
for the Organisation
she died for love
Is it far, he asks
meaning the boat
they've come to catch
his last words
We've a long way
to go, she says
then shoots
sending them
on their way
or is it
the Kingdom come
to them

Dada(III)

I didn't like
Breton's face
you couldn't
trust it
whereas Duchamp
made comedy deadly
For Picabia
beauty made sense
and Tzara was
a haircut away
from death
Dada had no future
and no past
and to its credit
though it was a gift
no present

The Color Red

Not only James Dean's
windbreaker
Natalie Wood is wearing
a red coat with a red ribbon
at the police station
where Dean and Sal Mineo
are also being held
Dean asks, "Do you think
I'm funny?"
Rebel Without A Cause
is red
from beginning to end
it's the color
of suffering
which
        unlike the movie
never ends

Lost Postcard

Turned on TV no sound
there it was black and white
a guy and a girl in a car
driving swervy fast in rain
at night his long fingers
spidery gesturing front of
riverine window the blonde
in tears tilted beret
feeling for door handle
threatening to jump—
it's America, honey
or used to be
which is why
I came back

Frank Jackson

In my dream someone asked me if
I remembered Frank Jackson
Hearing this name brought tears
to my eyes though I've never
known anyone by that name
an ordinary name
that made me cry
and think of being in a pub
in London fifty years ago
with a friend's girlfriend
soon to become his wife
They were older than I
and I can still picture her
wearing a fake mink coat
with short dark brown hair
and long earrings
a beautiful woman with a child
from her then-husband
who beat her, a poet I was told
She left him to marry my friend
but she became an alcoholic
liked drugs too much so later
my friend divorced her
and her son died young
of a drug overdose
Now she's in a nursing home
her mind mostly gone
she was a little wild and funny
and kind always to me
I went twice with her
to visit my friend when he was
in prison, first in the Scrubs
then in Maidstone—I suppose
I was a little in love with her

when I was twenty which is why
I'm writing this now about her
not Frank Jackson

The Difference

It's two days before Christmas
and the world has taken
a turn for the worse
as it always does
My thoughts on this rainy morning
are of those persons lingering
in my dreams
how they enter or leave uninvited
If they're trying to tell
me something I'd like
to know what it is
Do they choose to appear?
Are they looking for me?
A few nights ago in an airport
I thought I recognized someone
walking by I'd not seen
in seven years
She didn't notice me
or if she did
she didn't recognize me
Later I saw her sitting at a table
eating an ice cream cone
Her face was unblemished,
unwrinkled, completely white
she looked at me but said nothing
Which of us the ghost?

Edith Piaf Regrets Nothing

You didn't want me to go
with you to the Chopard dinner
Only rich people will be there
people who do nothing
but travel to the same places
with each other's wives
or husbands you'll be bored
I'd love to go, I said
Stay next to me these women
have faces of two day old fish
the men are lizards
Perhaps someone will jump
from the rooftop
of the Hotel Martinez
How do you like these
earrings?

With Dan at the Museum

On the 7th floor of the Whitney Museum
people pass or pause in front of
DeKooning's "Door to the River"
become part of the painting,
moving parts—
I've had a postcard of it on my
studio door for years,
I see it every day—
I'm also part of it
The postcard is faded,
bruised, discolored—faces
like rocks in the river—
like mine

Camera Oscura

I read today about an Italian painter
who at the close of the 19th century left Italy
and travelled to South America where he
remained for six years, then returned to Europe
Three years later he again travelled
to South America, this time to a remote part
of Paraguay to photograph an indigenous tribe
he had encountered and lived among
during his previous sojourn—
He disappeared after entering the Gran Chaco
and a year later his worm-infested corpse
was discovered rotting in the forest
decapitated, skull broken apart by stone axes
his cameras gone—
Many years later negatives of his photos
were found, developed and displayed, then published
What had he done to occasion his own demise?
Was his death worth the pictures he took?
Did members of the tribe suspect that he was
stealing their souls as plains Indians
and Tibetans did? Perhaps they took his cameras
away with them to try to figure out how to do it
or maybe buried them so they no longer could
be used to empty others—I think they took
the cameras apart in search of their souls
Who could blame them?

Cela ne fait rien

Our first date was at
La Closerie des Lilas
Do you still have the poem
I wrote for you on a napkin?
It's raining a little today,
unusual for June in California
Old times, you said, seeing
the photographs
You used to make fun of me
when I'd say, What difference
does it make? Do you remember?
It's dangerous to remember
so much, especially for a writer
The temptation to make sense
of it is always there
where you and I
are no longer

A Sunday Afternoon on the Island of Natural Things

A guy riding a bicycle
down the middle of a street
repeatedly shouting "hello!"
Shylock's daughter steals from him
a turquoise ring given her father
by his dead wife and trades it
for a monkey
A man I've never seen before
asks me how I am today
then answers himself
with the question
"Did God tell you?"
Is he the one burning down
buildings in my neighborhood?
Or could it be that guy
on the bicycle riding quickly
across the Rialto bridge
shouting "Hello!" to a girl
with a monkey on her shoulder?

My Books

My shelves are full of books
by dead men and women
Most of the authors
thought they had something
important to say
about what was going on
around them or only
in their own minds
The books contain truths,
lies, and every kind of
foolish thought, even
some not so foolish
What's to be done with them
if there no longer are readers?
About my own books, the ones
I've written, I'm not worried
They're going with me,
and a few of the others, too
I'll have plenty of room,
just as I've always had

What Bobby D. Taught Me

Robert Duncan was a great poet—
his poem "My Mother Was a Falconress"
is definitely part of the canon—
Bobby D., as our friend David Bromige,
also a great poet, used to call him—
they're both gone now—
I remember Duncan coming out
of a bookstore in San Francisco
running down the street shouting
to me, "Wait! Wait!" wanting
a ride back to his house—
In my car he said, "Make haste,
my dear Patroclos!"
"What's that?" I asked—
"Achilles, calling out from his ship
anchored in the harbor to Nestor,
onshore in his chariot. *The Iliad*,
dear Barry"—which sent me to Homer.

On Time

A few nights ago I was at the Oakland airport
waiting to pick up Mary Lou who was arriving from Denver
when an organist stationed in the combined lobby
and baggage claim to entertain the people
coming and going and sitting and standing around
began playing the theme from the old Perry Mason TV show
which was popular in the 1950s and '60s when I was a kid.
Hearing it cut through the dozen or so one-sided
cell phone conversations and PA announcements
I'd been trying to ignore enabled me to notice
Raymond Burr, Barbara Hale, Ray Collins, William Talman
and William Hopper, the stars of Perry Mason
gathered together at the belt depositing luggage
off a plane just in from Burbank.
"Have you been waiting long?" Mary Lou asked
when she appeared. "Not too long, I don't think,"
I answered, "time isn't the same as it used to be,
or else we're not. How was your flight?"
"Fine," she said, "it went by so fast."
"I know what you mean," I said.

No king in Israel

At my father's funeral
I was twelve years old
My father's brother
took me by the shoulders
standing in front of the open coffin
and said, Look at your father—
I did, for a moment, then turned away—
Several years later, when I read
Camus' novel, *L'Etranger*,
his description of the nurse
who'd attended Meursault's
dying mother in an old people's home,
hiding her leprosy with a white bandage
wrapped around her face below the eyes
to cover where her nose had been,
it reminded me of my father
as he was in his coffin,
wrapped with death, nothing left
for me—

Utah Street

This would have been a perfect late morning
to call my old pal Jerry Rosen and have a conversation
Foggy, cool, listening to "K.C. Blues"
Charlie Parker blowing on his birthday
Jerry would know without my telling him
but he's not around any more other than
in the air and my thoughts—
He was one of the people who believed in me,
my work, without self-comparison, understanding
we're all different, writers, reaching for
our own voices—but that's small potatoes,
it was his great suffering heart that mattered—
This poem, not really a poem, is for myself,
Jerry reminding me how important continue
asking for too much, how else find something,
anything worth keeping, like the time wanting
to explain I wrote a whole chapter of a novel
sitting on his porch on Utah Street in San Francisco
with the front door open while he plunked Monk
one-handed on the piano and when I came in
put on Anita O'Day record "Tenderly"
he smiled, said, "I understand"

Reverdy

Have I ever told you
why I'm enamored of
the poems of Pierre Reverdy?
It's because besides flinging
images impossible
to imagine they're numbers
that don't add up or mean
anything,
yet often when
I set down a cup on an
uneven surface, spilling
its contents a little,
or the sky is uncertain
I'm reminded of
Reverdy's reckless accuracy
without looking

Bad Blonde

Driving in night snowstorm
Denver to Cheyenne
January 1968
    in '64 white Pontiac
      with 16 year old
        runaway girl
stole her daddy's gun—
    I was 21, didn't think twice
    about doing anything
    other than what seemed
    right at the time
    not knowing no time
    if it's really right
    ever comes again

New Mexico, 1969

In March of that year, when we were both twenty-two,
my friend Paul and I drove from San Francisco to New Mexico,
forty-six years after D.H. Lawrence first was there.
We stayed with people in Ranchos de Taos who lived
in an adobe house on a dusty, deeply rutted, dirt road.
There was much hostility in Taos: Anglo ranchers
who hated Hispanics, Hispanics who hated hippies
and bikers who hated each other, and Apaches and Navajos
who hated everyone other than their own—about them
Lawrence remarked, "The Indians are much more remote
than Negroes." Paul and I were exploring, looking for
a new place to live—we swam amid the ruins of an old hotel
in a river seven thousand feet above sea level that ran
through the magnificent Sangre de Cristo mountains
observed by a large puma. In 1922, Lawrence wrote
to a friend in England, "America lives by a sort of
egoistic will, shove and be shoved," and declared,
"I will not be shoved." Seven years later he died in France.
One afternoon I followed a group of self-flagellating
Penitentes crawling on their knees up a rugged road
to a cemetery—watching them I remembered what Lawrence
wrote there: "The dead don't die. They look on and help."
Paul and I stayed for a couple of weeks, then went back
to California.

Neruda

Did the poet die
of cancer or
was he murdered
twelve days after
the coup d'etat
He was an enemy
of the new regime
considered dangerous
as all poets are
or should be
Thirty-four years
after the poet's death
can this question
be answered with certainty
There is always
another question
to be asked
and given his or her
unfortunate contract
drawn up at birth
by a bad lawyer
rarely is there
an answer a poet
can accept

The Cause

When the Russian writer Anton Chekhov
worked as a census taker in Sakhalin
he encountered a man who said he had been
for many years a prisoner in the Gulag
and claimed to be a son of Simón Bolívar,
the self-proclaimed liberator of South America—
This man told Chekhov that after his father's
death he had come to Russia from Venezuela
to raise money to continue his father's struggle
to organize an effort to consolidate all of
Latin America into one country to be called Amerarcana—
Chekhov could not speak Spanish but neither could
this son of Bolívar who claimed to have lost
all memory of his native language during
his many years at hard labor and could now
speak only Russian except for one sentence:
"Yo soy un hombre de Caracas"—
Chekhov gave him a few pennies for his cause
and saw him only once more, stumbling drunkenly
down a snowy street, his long beard a tangle
of icicles—Chekhov described this man in his diary
and made a note to write a story about him
entitled "The Cause" but never did.

Thy Own Hand Yields Thy Death's Instrument, Sez Ez

Pound was crazy
from his early years
used erudition
to allay his fears
grandiosity trumped precocity
but not pomposity
For fascism fell
axe bundled with sticks
descent into hell
he couldn't fix
Imaginary Chinese
and ancient Greeks
more than these
creepy freaks
to his bughouse crawled
dispatched them all
to commit such crimes
as from earlier times
An ideogrammatic excuse
was what he invented
nothing, he claimed
could be prevented
Even his poems
came bizarre and bad
a tired brain
a face gone sad
In the end his silence
spoke the only way
admit never having
had his own
words to say

The Chinese Pastoral Society

Five-thirty in the morning
I see an old lady
sleeping on the ground
in front of the door
to the Chinese Pastoral Society
in Oakland, California,
her one blanket down
around her knees
I pull it up over her shoulders
she doesn't move
The Chinese Pastoral Society,
of course, is closed
I look more closely
at her face
She's Asian, could be fifty,
sixty, even seventy or eighty
years old—
The word pastoral has several
meanings, the most common
of which pertains to
shepherds or their way of life,
rural, rustic, idealized
as peaceful, simple and natural,
but this society must have to do
with pastors, ministers, churches
Nothing on the door or
front window gives any
explicit information
There is pastoral literature, too,
dealing with life in the country
And pastorales, operas and cantatas
suggesting an unpretentious,
idyllic life—
This homeless woman must have

come for help, not music,
poems or plays describing farms
or children running unfettered
through open fields
in bright sunshine—
An old lady
lying on a dirty sidewalk
in a city before dawn
I put a ten dollar bill
next to her left hand
under the thin blanket
Nothing else to do
but let her sleep,
perhaps dreaming of
two Chinese poets hiking,
arguing about which mountain
is the more beautiful

What She Did Have

The best thing about her
was how she walked,
undulating, slow waves
never hurrying, a ship
on the ocean, steady wind
propelling an unvarying
advance, signifying
purpose—
Pretty, too, though
her upper lip, permanently
curled, conveyed contempt
and disdain regardless
of intent—
a hopeless *arriviste*
for whom I could have
no lasting affection,
but watching her walk
kept my attention

Myth without Text

It was in Rome that I saw
the most beautiful girl
standing on a sidewalk talking
to her friends, schoolmates,
all of them no more than sixteen
or seventeen years old—
this one stood out from the rest,
black hair and eyes, porcelain skin,
she glowed amid dirty air,
rambunctious traffic, surly passersby—
And here I was, fifty-two years old,
stunned by this face,
Cassiopeia to Helen to her—
Ambushed by Beauty, I fled
like Creon of Thebes from
the uncatchable Cadmeian vixen

Thanksgiving 2017

We were gathered on the stone steps
leading up to the main house
family and friends, Mary Lou and I
Phoebe, Kevin and Rachelina
Asa, Antoinette with Asaiah and Amarin
Randi and Marcus and Damon, Mary
Amanda and Del, Vinnie, my brother
Marky, Oscar and Rebecca, Cole and Max
Kev and Elissa, Peter and Jane
everyone there for the holiday
even Claudia and her three kids
from France, talking and laughing
when someone shouted to me
Barry, look, it's your father
and there he was, wearing a brown suit
with a wide red tie, looking
just as he did in 1957, the year
before he died, when I was eleven
and my brother was five
I turned to Marky and said
Marky, come on, Dad's here
I want to introduce you to him

3-7-77

Three feet wide, seven feet deep,
seventy-seven inches long—
my maternal grandmother's home
for the same length of time
that she was alive—
I have a photograph of her
when she was three or four
years old, 1895 or '96, in Chicago,
a few years after her parents
and her sister fled from Constantinople
to America—
Her name was Rose, she played piano
and sang, taught me to follow notes
on sheet music, how to keep time—
She had two husbands that I know of,
lots of boyfriends—she died
when I was eight—I know the face
in the photo taken almost
sixty years earlier—
When I was the same age she is
in that picture, at her house
in Florida, she gave me a toy gun
and said it was for me to protect
her and my mother—
I carried that little pistol
everywhere I went while
I was there—I have a photograph
of myself holding it, standing
in front of a palm tree—
Both Rose and my mother
are long gone now, but no harm
came to them on my watch

Literature

I suppose it's true
there are things one never
gets over or past
certain people and events
war, the holocaust, failed
relationships, friendships
that end badly, deaths
To survive is not always
a choice, of course
and seldom is there a cure
for feelings or memories
that haunt and disturb
best to accept and learn
how to live with them
James Joyce wrote, "Certainly
she remembers the past. All
women do." All animals
remember, not just women
but he was making a point
And do these memories
disappear when we do
I can only assume so
which is why there
is literature

My Dream

Woke up 5 A.M.
put on Dexter Gordon record
"Stairway to the Stars"
stumbling, sky still dark
My dream—swimming in a warm sea
somewhere in Europe
Italy, I think
or Dalmatian coast
A voice asking
Are you there?
a woman's voice
not one I recognize
I look around, treading water
forest at island's shore
Is this where the voice
is coming from?
Circe calling from her house
of smooth stone?
Better not to know
or hear more
than Dexter's horn

She Had A Beautiful Voice

Sitting alone on a bench
in Washington Square Park
scribbling in notebook
Old Chinese guy sits down
near me steals my newspaper
as I write disappears it
in his navy blue peacoat
He smokes doesn't look at me
his handskin like
potsticker dough
he gets up walks away
Dead bird on sidewalk
a sparrow
second day of October
my favorite month
the last good weather
You're far away—
stay there

Rough Mix for Miles Okazaki

More and more I listen to Monk
"Functional" of course
takes your mind
down the river
in a canoe that doesn't
quite tip over
then the almost 22 minute
version of "Round Midnight"
not letting up
before "Monk's Mood"
demands your attention
for the rest of the afternoon
Writing about music
makes no sense unless
you already know it
In Monk's case
there's no dénouement
only one rentrée
after another
begin again and hold
that thought until
you don't need to

Finding Favor in the Sight of the King

There's a great photo by Ralph Eugene Meatyard
of four black kids shooting craps on a city sidewalk
in winter or late fall I'd guess because
they're wearing sweaters, coats and caps
taken in the mid-1950s, black and white
around the time my mother taught me
and my cousin Chris how to play craps
on the sidewalk in front of his house in Chicago
I must have been seven years old, Chris eleven
The three of us were kneeling down throwing dice
when his mother came out of the house
and furiously accused my mother of corrupting us
I remember the two women shouting at each other
My aunt was older than my mother who was
in her twenties, she was laughing
stood up, put the dice into her purse
got into her Buick convertible and drove away
Chris's mother made him go inside with her
I could have been with those kids
in Meatyard's photograph instead of
left alone on the sidewalk but you know
my mother was fun to be around in those days

Weekend

A weekend was all it was
and since then we haven't spoken
You were the one who embraced me
on the top floor
your kiss a surprise
your right leg wrapped around my left
A weekend with a zany interlude
in a Mexican drugstore
to make sure you wouldn't
get pregnant
We ate well, visited a friend
You drove me to the airport
got lost on the way
Call me when you get there
you said, another surprise
I did, left a message
Reverdy wrote, No one knows
where time will stop
Or, he was wise enough
to omit, memory

Montana

We were walking next
　　to the river—
　　Where are we? you asked
　　Montana, I said,
the Big Sky state,
　　　　far north—
A long way from Paris,
　　　　you said
Yes, a very long way—
　　You are glad to see me?
　　Yes, certainly—
Do you still believe
　　we have no chance?
What could make me
　　believe otherwise?
A fish jumped up out of
the river and almost landed
　　on the bank—
　　Such a crazy fish,
　　　　you said, it would die
　　　　out of the water, yes?
We kept walking, then
　　a cold breeze came
　　and you shivered—
I understand, you said,
　I shouldn't be here,
　I'll go back to Paris—
Neither of us got much
　　sleep that night—
A year later you called
　　and said, I want to come—
I'll be in Alabama, going
　fishing with an old friend—
Remember how the fish

jumped from the river
almost to me?
Where was that? you asked,
there were mountains—
Montana—
I liked it there, you said,
it was beautiful

The Lion Dying Thrusteth
Forth His Paw

Up early before the sun
as on most days these days
After coffee, fruit, toast
watched *House of Bamboo*
on TV while reading *La prisonnière*
Not thinking about gang
of ex-GI criminals operating
in Tokyo 1954, or Proust's boys
but about my granddaughters,
how smart they are, how talented
and beautiful and how much
I love them—I want to live
a long time, long enough to see
what they do with their lives,
to meet their children, to know
their names and memorize their faces—
Everything I've done, everywhere
I've been, all the people I've known,
none of it will mean anything
to them, and even less to me

The Arm

My friend Patrick has a friend
whose right arm was pulled off
by an orangutan—
The guy is a terrible driver,
Patrick says, goes too fast,
insists on driving a car
with a stick shift, part of
his trying to prove
that missing an arm
is no impediment
to his physical skills—
He was an animal handler
at a zoo, the orangutan
loved him and one day
wouldn't let go, fought
to keep the arm until
he was tranquilized
and it was taken away—
The arm could not be
surgically reattached—
When the orangutan saw the man again
he began jumping up and down
and screeching, reaching
for him through the bars
of his cage—
Let him out, said the man,
he wants to embrace me,
but the zookeeper would not
and led the man away—
Before this incident, Patrick
told me, the orangutan
was always happy to have visitors,
jabbering at them, cavorting
around, but now he appears

despondent, mostly sits
and doesn't eat much—
What happened to the arm?
I asked—My friend kept it,
Patrick said, preserved in a freezer—
every so often he takes out the arm
and looks at it, but he's stopped
going to see the orangutan—
He feels guilty, he says, as if
he had pulled off his own arm

Le Dénouement

I remember rain
    our walking away
   from each other
    arguing again,
     impatient
as though we had forever
  as though
    there ever
  were forever—
   Sibyl
with the Latin face
   somebody said,
      best
     recognizable
    by moonlight
none of it made me
a better person—
  A year
after we'd stopped
  (I had, anyway)
  a friend said
    to me,
  You're much nicer
     now,
everybody says so—
I was not flattered
nor did I believe
  this to be true
  (I still don't)
  I was angry,
    that's all—
  failure had made
    it seem so

American Pastime

When I was a little kid in Chicago
Jimmy Yancey, the great blues
and boogie-woogie piano player,
worked as a groundskeeper
at Comiskey Park, where the White Sox played—
Years later, I listened to his records
and did the best I could to imitate
his left hand, not knowing he'd played
baseball for the Chicago All-Americans
in the Negro Leagues, throwing down
his best curves and sliders on both
the black and white keys, remembering
how he'd appeared as a tap dancer
and pianist in Europe and at Carnegie Hall,
then kept his day job working at Comiskey
for twenty-five years, until he died
in 1951, sweeping the infield

Immortals

In 1952, Virgil Trucks, a pitcher
for the Detroit Tigers, won only
five games and lost nineteen—
however, of the five he won
two were complete game no-hitters,
one against the lowly Washington Senators,
the other against the mighty World champion
New York Yankees at Yankee Stadium—
An earlier Virgil, author of The Aeneid,
about whom the poet Statius wrote,
in the voice of Dante, "The seeds of my ardor
were the sparks from that divine flame
whereby more than a thousand have kindled,
I speak of The Aeneid, mother to me
and nurse to me in poetry"—
On those two afternoons in May and August
long past myth and time, it was
the later Virgil from whose flaming
right arm sparks flew, throwing seeds
out of phantom motion created poetry
perfect enough to render opponents
helpless as those immortalized men of Troy.

The Most Dangerous Age

Borges is the Vega, the falling
vulture of Latin literature, or
the leopard, crouched on a branch
of the tree, awaiting further
instruction from Cervantes,
asleep on the highest limb,
under no pressure to wake up—
Seated on the ground below
are Marquez, Mutis, Cortázar,
maybe Bolaño, if he's not
still alive—all with this
understanding, that nothing
belongs to them other than
blindness and their varying
ability to handle a knife

Ambush

Wild woman with gun
Shoots 4 then Self
headline in
this morning's paper
Why only some words
capitalized? Why Shoots
not woman or gun?
I turned on TV movie
Ambush (1949) Robert Taylor
as scout tracking down
enemy Apache chief Diablito
took hostage Arlene Dahl's
sister—Dahl couldn't act
but Taylor no doubt
discovered what she
could do—worlds and more
than time from today's
headline Diablito couldn't
read but he could kill
White men were taking
his land—the woman who
shot four people ambushed
them at their workplace
she must have thought
she had something to lose

Midnight Makes Its Move

Lee Konitz on alto, 1955,
with Lennie Tristano's piano
in the Sing Song Room
of The Confucius Restaurant
New York City, you can hear
everything that can be
expected without too much
rouge or lipstick, just
the goods—Perfection,
close to it, anyway, nothing
hidden in plain sight
or sound, a ghost of a chance
as there always is, and
they took it this summer
night in a chop suey joint
mid-'50s Manhattan when
for some of us these are
all the things there are

Turn Again and Tell the Captain

Three great elegies in modern jazz—
Lennie Tristano's "Requiem" for Charlie Parker
    (Tristano's solo recording)
Benny Golson's "I Remember Clifford" for
Clifford Brown (recordings by Donald Byrd
    on trumpet, Bud Powell on piano)
Charlie Mingus's "Goodbye Pork Pie Hat"
for Lester Young (Mingus recording)—
Many other laments exist, of course,
most I've never heard, but these
are right there in my head—
I prefer music to poems, words don't
live the same way—so, listen.

How Chet Baker Died

I saw Chet Baker in the early 1970s
at Stryker's, a small jazz club
off Amsterdam Avenue on the upper West Side
of Manhattan, in the middle
of a harsh winter
I walked over from where I was staying
on 85th and Riverside Drive,
a weekday night, braving wind and snow
curious to hear what he sounded like
a few years after he'd had his front teeth
knocked out by drug dealers in San Francisco
I knew he'd been living in Italy
where he'd been in jail but become
a living legend
Miles Davis hated him famously
because of his good looks (now gone)
and popularity despite his rudimentary technique
There were perhaps twelve people in the club
including myself—Chet Baker came onstage
wearing a brown sportcoat, no tie, blue slacks,
slicked back hair, caved-in cheeks,
put trumpet to lips and blew—
there it was, that flat, sweet tone
but without sustaining notes the way
he had before losing his own teeth
I've forgotten the sidemen—piano, bass
and drums—or any tunes other than
The Touch of Your Lips, Travelin' Light
and These Foolish Things
I went back the next night and there
were about thirty-five people in the audience
Baker was wearing the same clothes, he
didn't say much—I left after the second set
He died not too long after, fell out

of a window in Amsterdam, maybe he was pushed
a junkie's demise—I remember the weather
better than I do his performances
Ernest Hemingway's advice to young writers
was to not forget the weather
and I haven't

Forward and Back

Fifty-four years ago
almost no money in my pockets
I arrived in Paris
duffel bag over one shoulder,
a guitar, no place to stay,
slept in train station waiting rooms,
under bridges—cops stopped me
to inspect papers, make sure
I had valid passport, told them
I'd been working as ordinary seaman
on ship—eighteen years old—
Walking past bookshop on rue de l'Odeon
in window I saw copies of famous
literary journal La Nouvelle Revue Française
founded 1908 by André Gide, photos of
Camus, Colette, Reverdy, Flaubert, Sartre
on covers—wondered how I could get
from where I was, fledgling writer
no credits to my name, to where
they were—When it happened
twenty-five years later, seeing
my name on NRF cover felt strange,
almost as if it were a different person,
not only from who I was then but before,
kid carrying dirty green seabag
and guitar—Reverdy wrote, "il est entré
à la place de celui qu'on attendait"
("he made his entry, taking the place
of the one who was awaited")

Beyond the Rivers of Ethiopia

There is a photograph of Ernest Hemingway
with Errol Flynn taken in La Floridita,
Hemingway's favorite bar in Havana—
The men look very old, though the writer
was only sixty, the actor almost fifty—
Both would be dead within months,
Flynn in Vancouver, B.C., with his
sixteen year old girlfriend, Hemingway
in Idaho punching out his own lights—
They were heavy drinkers, certainly,
and chasers—Errol of women, Ernest
to control the way everyone behaved
and thought, especially of him—
Having outlived themselves in these
vainest of pursuits, they went crazy,
Hemingway's brain wired to electrical critics
with whom he could not argue, Flynn filming
himself and the nymphet in *Cuban Rebel Girls*,
a movie never released—After hearing
of the death of his famous customer,
the bartender in La Floridita told
a reporter for the *Havana Post*,
Success kills everyone who has it.
We will name a cocktail after him.

Special Collections

You held the letters
from James to Conrad
and Hawthorne to Melville
as though they were
precious stones brought out
of the Congo at the expense
of a dozen lives,
or priceless pearls prised
from oysters by naked boy
divers on the floor
of a Polynesian lagoon—
Astonished the library
allowed us to handle
and read these treasures,
as you called them,
you said, They really
must trust you—
Yes, I said, now maybe
you will, too

Jim Harrison

for Mary Lou

I miss Jim Harrison,
not just his new poems and novels
he won't write,
his blind, wandering left eye,
gargantuan appetite, his generosity—
He loved Mary Lou's flowers,
sitting in our garden—
He'd never been to a racetrack
so I took him, taught him
how to read The Racing Form,
how to bet—we both won
a little that day—
He'd call me after midnight,
I could hear the ice clink
in his glass of Scotch
before the gravelly voice—
He'd never fail to mention
Mary Lou's flowers in letters,
on the phone and when we met—
When I was in my twenties
he told me, "If you lived in New York
you'd already be a famous poet."
Walking on his property near
the Arizona-Mexico border
he brushed away a rattlesnake
with his cane—"I don't
shoot snakes any more," he said,
"unless I have to, like writing poems."
He died two years ago.
Mary Lou's flowers are beautiful
this year, Jim, especially
the blue irises.

Great Expectations

Only in dreams is it possible
to wait for the dead to return—
In two dreams last night
I found myself where I did not belong,
places and situations to which
I'd returned only to encounter
difficulties impossible to avoid—
in both cases I became desperate
and attempted to leave but was delayed
by hostile people and bad weather—
The mistake I'd made was to have
gone back, and made worse because
neither person I'd hoped to see appeared.
When finally I was able to escape,
I twice woke up knowing I had only
myself to blame, the second time
more disgusted than disappointed—
It was light outside, so I stayed up,
put on Ben Webster *King of the Tenor
Saxophone*—halfway through "Tenderly"
I began to feel better, sat down
at the kitchen table and wrote,
"Don't expect anything from the dead."

Colorado

One of my favorite movies is Colorado Territory
(1949, directed by Raoul Walsh) starring Joel McCrea
and Virginia Mayo—McCrea is Wes McQueen, a robber
and killer, Mayo's a half-breed ex-dancehall girl
hooked up with a no-good desperado—her name
is Colorado—"I was born under a chuck wagon,"
she tells McQueen, with whom she falls in love,
"and I ain't never got any higher"—After a train
hold-up goes wrong McCrea and Mayo head for the hills,
an Anasazi cliff dwelling, where they're hunted down
by the law—This is a remake of High Sierra, in which
Bogart and Ida Lupino go on the lam—both men
have other women they wanted, but nothing works out
for anyone, especially these boys—Mayo makes the most
of her time and has the best scene where she digs
a bullet out of McCrea's shoulder and cauterizes
the wound with gunpowder she ignites with a match—
Neither of the good girls the boys are after turn out
to be good, it's Mayo and Lupino who are the stand-up
chicks—Mayo's sexy and nasty like she was in White Heat
with Cagney, but here she's got Indian blood in her face,
native smarts and honest intentions, so she steals
the show—Mayo never became a big star but she could
play dirty, which in these kinds of movies is all
she needed to be remembered 70 years later in a poem.

Isolation

When Charlie Parker
playing "Ko Ko" comes on the radio
it's unmistakable, changes
the furniture around in your head—
Bird broke across a border
nobody knew was there,
like Babe Ruth did in baseball
Buddha in India
Jules Verne on the moon—
The visceral effect
Parker's "Ko Ko" has on a listener
is comparable to that
a viewer gets watching
Elisha Cook, Jr., being gunned down
in *Shane* when he flies backwards
parallel to the ground
and lands in the muddy street—
There goes Charlie, faster, tougher,
trickier, taking the air
out of the enormous room
he's been in since 1955—
Does he know nobody's around
who can hear him?

4 A.M. Used to Be Night, Now it's Morning

Falling in love
is like listening
to Johnny Hodges
on alto playing
"What's the Rush?"
don't think about
what's coming
next

A Love Story for Nelson Algren

His name was Davey Fuqua, from Paris, Tennessee—
When I met him he worked in Chicago digging graves
after being dishonorably discharged from the army
for killing another GI in their barracks—
The soldier Davey killed was drunk when he came in
one night and saw Davey showing a photograph
of a woman to someone—The drunken soldier looked
at the photo and said, Who's that whore?
Davey cold cocked him and the guy hit his head
against the metal bar at the foot of a bunk—
Davey explained to the sergeant in charge
that he was holding a picture of his ex-wife
who'd run off with another man when the drunk
came in and said what he said—Davey was still
in love with her, they had a two year old daughter,
and kept the photo with him during his six months
in the stockade—After he was released he found out
where his ex-wife and her new husband were living
and that night climbed up a drainpipe on the outside
of their house and broke a window to get in—
The husband had a loaded shotgun pointed at Davey
when he went back out the window—
Davey began using heroin, then stole a Cadillac
from a dealership, drove it out through
the showroom window intending to kidnap his ex-wife
and daughter and take them with him to Tennessee
but ran out of gas with the cops on his tail—
He did a year at Joliet and died two weeks later
with a needle in his arm—When his ex-wife heard
the news she took her daughter and disappeared—
Her husband found them months later living in
a trailer in Arkansas—he begged her to go back
with him to Chicago but she refused, so he left
and never saw her again—Her name was Theresa.

Conchita

I'm staying in a room on the top floor
of a hotel on a quiet street in New Orleans
that was once a Catholic church
The restaurant and bar are in
what was formerly the rectory
The rooms are slightly monastic
as one might expect
modest, tasteful, comfortable, too
with a big bay window
and crossed (of course) wooden beams
Sitting in a chair at midnight
taking off my shoes
I glanced up at the beam
running the length of the short side
of the room over the bed
and there, carved in lower case letters,
is the name *conchita*—
The hotel has been open for only
a brief time, so I doubt that
the carving was done by a guest
For a few years after the church
closed its doors the building
was abandoned—possibly Conchita
was the name of a squatter
temporarily in residence
Could Conchita have been a parishioner?
I prefer to think so
a rebellious girl looking for kicks,
not faith or guidance
I'll call this Conchita's Cuarto
picturing her on her knees
a priest stroking her long, silky black hair
Conchita's tears staining his hassock
as he prays aloud for her deliverance

Or perhaps there's more to the story
she was a priest's secret
his imprisoned mistress
whom he hid, fed and protected
in this corner of a House of God—
were only Conchita here
with me now to confess

Homage to Simonides

Rimbaud wrote
I is somebody else
(Je est un autre)
a precise response
to those who attribute
fiction to experience
(which Wilde defined
as mistakes)
though that was not
all the poet meant—
In his story
Funes the memorioso
Borges furnished Funes
the opinion that dreams
are a waste of time
I disagree
a privilege reserved
for the living
as if the dead
have none

At Giza

Nine years ago saw sun set
facing Sphinx at Giza,
surprised how small
lion with head of man,
not female of Thebes
whose riddle Oedipus solved,
kept his head and became king—
this symbol of morning sun
called Harmachis—
only a few people around,
wondered what architects expected
or Pharaoh—reminded me
of Lipschitz's winged sculpture
Oscar Wilde's tomb at Pére-Lachâise—
Human beings born frightened,
die frightened—
statues, monuments, myths, magic,
nothing without imagination
our only saving grace—
Paul chastised the Athenians
building idols to an unknown god,
desperation personified, falling
to pieces like everything else

Bologna

In Bologna we had the ugliest hotel room,
large but with hideous wallpaper, brown and white checks,
and drapes the shade of Mississippi mud—
We had martinis dry in the downstairs bar, very strong,
and the bartender sang for us something from an opera
you recognized—I was there to appear at the Cineteca
on the Piazzetta Pier Paolo Pasolini, whom you knew
when you were a child—At midnight movies were shown
outdoors on a wall in the city's center—
Padre Pio had recently been given sainthood,
pictures of him were displayed everywhere—
We fought as always, nothing different there,
though we were rescued by humor, our saving grace—
It rained every day, making the cobblestones slippery,
the food was good—A few years later I was back
in Bologna, without you, but I felt like
a Mescalero Apache in southern Arizona in 1863
sneaking through the streets knowing the end
of my life was near— When someone asked me
why I didn't seem to be having a good time,
I replied, If you've ever been pinned down
in the desert with a dead horse, you'd know.

Rinchu

In 1975, when I was 28, I met Rinchu,
a guy about my age, in Sapporo, Japan—
he was a friend of people I'd met in Tokyo,
communards who lived in Kokubunji-shi,
young people who opposed ordinary standards
of behavior, the first fully grown generation
of post-World War II Japanese, those
not shamed or humbled by their country's
loss of the war—
Rinchu dressed like a Samurai, a long, dark robe
tied with a bright sash at his waist, in which
he brazenly carried a big knife, he wore sandals
and had long hair sometimes tied up in a bun
but most often flowing loose, covering
his shoulders, also a drooping mustache
and thin beard—he was tall for a Japanese man,
my height, with a sturdy build—
We traveled together through the Hokkaido
countryside, heading north on foot,
avoiding cities as much as possible—
Rinchu enjoyed flouting customs, such as
not eating while walking in public—he ate
apples and tossed their cores by the side
of the road, laughing in the faces
of offended strangers—Rinchu liked
being a rebel in his conflicted, confusing
country, as he described it, a place
no longer old and not young, unsure of itself—
Emperor Hirohito still alive in seclusion,
a man once considered God, now without honor,
whom most citizens felt should have committed
seppuku following the Japanese surrender—
One day Rinchu and I encountered an old man
carrying a load of sticks on his back,

bent over so far that the tip of his stringy
white beard almost touched the ground—
he appeared suddenly from thick woods
bordering the dirt road we were hiking on,
to me a character out of a storybook—
Rinchu greeted him using words I didn't understand,
telling me he'd addressed the man as
an "ancient wanderer"—the old man mumbled
as he passed by, making Rinchu laugh—"Lost boys"
he called us, said Rinchu—We parted on
a gravel road near Asahigawa, where I'd promised
to meet a friend—Rinchu told me he would continue
into the mountains "to stay lost, tomodachi,"
(which means friend) "for a while, anyway—
perhaps one day you will, too."

Mexican Waitress

I almost always like Mexican waitresses—
young or old they smile a lot and are eager
to refill a customer's coffee cup—
best is to sit on a stool at the counter
and carry on a conversation as she hurries
to put down plates of eggs, bowls of
menudo or pozole and pours more coffee—
A counter waitress I knew used to talk about
never getting married again even though
she was only nineteen—she had bleached
her hair blonde, she said, because Dionasio,
her husband, was always scoping out gueritas,
so to please him she changed the color,
hoping he'd look only at her—it didn't work,
Dionasio ran off with a blonde gringa
and left her broke in East L.A.
with a six month old baby and her black roots
starting to show—If I ever do get married
again, she added, it won't be to a Mexican
man, maybe a pelirrubio gringo who is
crazy for morenitas—Her name was Mistral,
she told me, given her because she was
born during a hurricane—What about you?
she asked, are you married? No, I answered,
but I have black hair—Yes, but you have
blue eyes, she said, that's good enough.

Mexican Haircut

Barbershop Jalapa, Mexico—
turn of last century hard cracked black leather
Chicago manufactured chairs reclined comfortably
as slick-coiffed barber began ministrations—
machete blade ceiling fans gently urging shredded hair
across black & white tiled floor—
Tita sat on a low stool at footrest looking up,
anaconda-ridden riverdark deep brown eyes
inspecting snip after snip, she and barber
chatting away too rapido for me to understand
accompaniment to pelaquero's scissors dance—
When I saw this place like in Traven's Tampico
1948 Treasure of the Sierra Madre movie
I had to go in, asked Cuanto para cortar el pelo?
Ochos pesos, almost a buck—remembering Bogart
when John Huston's white hat white-suited Americano
slaps two silver dollars into his outstretched palm,
after haircut hat didn't fit—Asked Tita,
How do I look? Muy guapo, she said, though the sides
felt uneven—Outside on the street hot sun burned
back of my powdered neck naked now—You give him
too much, Tita laughed, like Concha in Last Chance
Saloon, una propina grande—Well, I said, made him
happy, and I'm happy, too, with my Mexican haircut—

History Lesson

In the movie Laughing Boy (1934) there's nothing
to laugh about—
Lupe Velez, known as the Mexican Spitfire,
plays a beautiful Navaho girl
who's taken off the reservation
to a school in town where she learns
the ways of the white world—
She tries to live like a white woman
but falls prey to unscrupulous people
and is soon reduced to turning tricks—
Disgusted by her unwholesome existence
she returns to the reservation
and tries to become a good Navaho—
she charms an innocent brave
named Laughing Boy and convinces him
to marry her—
Laughing Boy is under her spell,
deludes himself into thinking
she'll be like other Navaho wives,
but Lupe falls back into her town habits—
She leaves the reservation and becomes
the personal whore of a rich rancher—
Laughing Boy finds her and shoots
an arrow at the rancher, but Lupe
gets in the way and takes the arrow
in her heart—
Dying, she professes her love
for Laughing Boy, tells him
she'll be waiting for him
on the Other Side—
He eludes capture and heads back
to the reservation where he asks
the moon and the mountains to keep him
from temptations of the white life,

promising the spirits to stay pure
for his reunion with the wife
whose heart was broken
by the white man's ways
that forced him to pierce it
with an arrow—
This is the history of America.

Swans

Achilles became King of the Dead,
denied to Odysseus the importance
of this distinction, said
he'd rather be alive though enslaved
to the cruelest of masters—
In life it's possible to be rescued
by imagination—There are no mysteries,
only what remains unknown,
and as we know, nothing remains,
which is probably why
in spring swans fly
to the west coast
of Ireland.

Sitting in the Sun Reading Chekhov

Sitting in the sun reading Chekhov.
One of his characters says, A woman
will forgive audacity and impudence
but never reasonableness—Years ago,
remarking about a young woman I soon
came to know very well, a mutual friend
said, She likes to have some danger
in her life. Chekhov never looked away
from the truth but he didn't find a need
to put his faith in it. There is
a question for which everyone wants
an answer, not realizing the consequence
if ever they get it. Our mutual friend
never read Chekhov, but he was right.

Early October Remembering
My Friend Toru Takemitsu

I keep
in
my apricot chest
the willow
branch
you gave me
the morning
we parted
at Peach Blossom
Spring
brittle now
I handle it
tenderly
How can it be
you are
no longer
there
to dangle
your fingers
in the bright
green
water

When I Am Walking

Often now, when
I am walking alone,
I have the feeling
others are with me—
I strain to hear
familiar voices,
but when they come
it's like cats making love
in an empty temple—
Perhaps they exist
only in my imagination,
nonetheless I am pleased
to be in their company—
The older I become
the more there is
to remember, so how is it
that to forget
feels as does
the coming of spring?

In a Past Life I Was
Mistakenly a Poet

When we lived in the mountains
my thoughts were simple
compared with those to come
Almost fifty years have passed
hair white
friends gone
More often alone
I forget the time
between then and now
Is it necessary to recapture
the past my only question
Autumn begins
I felt it yesterday morning
hiking by the bay
On my way back to the mountains
the wind's no longer
against me
Should I be surprised?

INDEX OF POEM TITLES

BARRY GIFFORD's first book of poems was *The Blood of the Parade*, published in London, England, in 1967. Since then he has published many poetry collections, the most recent being *Imagining Paradise: New and Selected Poems*. His fiction includes the novels *Landscape with Traveler, Wyoming, Sailor & Lula: The Complete Novels* and *The Roy Stories*. His film credits include *Wild at Heart, Perdita Durango, Lost Highway* and *The Phantom Father*. He lives in the San Francisco Bay Area. For more information visit www.barrygifford.net.